THESE ARE YOUR RIGHTS!

By Lena Rostock

Illustrated by Lotta Persson

Library For All Ltd.

Library For All is an Australian not for profit organisation with a mission to make knowledge accessible to all via an innovative digital library solution. Visit us at libraryforall.org

These Are Your Rights

This edition published 2022

Published by Library For All Ltd
Email: info@libraryforall.org
URL: libraryforall.org

This work is licensed under the Creative Commons Attribution-NonCommercial-NoDerivatives 4.0 International License. To view a copy of this license, visit http://creativecommons.org/licenses/by-nc-nd/4.0/.

Library For All gratefully acknowledges the contributions of all who made previous editions of this book possible.

This book was made possible by the generous support of Save The Children.

Save the Children

Original illustrations by Lotta Persson

These Are Your Rights
Rostock, Lena
ISBN: 978-1-922827-56-2
SKU02681

THESE ARE YOUR RIGHTS!

Hi everyone!
This book tells you about
your rights. These rights
are the same for all children.
Read, draw and talk about
them with your friends.

I am the Children's Dragon!

My name is

_____

My name is Julia!

I'm Oscar!

I am called Joseph!

And I'm called Minna

My name is _____.

All children are worth
the same.
You and me and all children
in the whole world.

I have the right to a family.

I have the right to learn
things in pre-school
and school.

I have the right to spend time with both my mother and my father.

I have the right
to say what I think.

I have the right to
get help when I am ill.

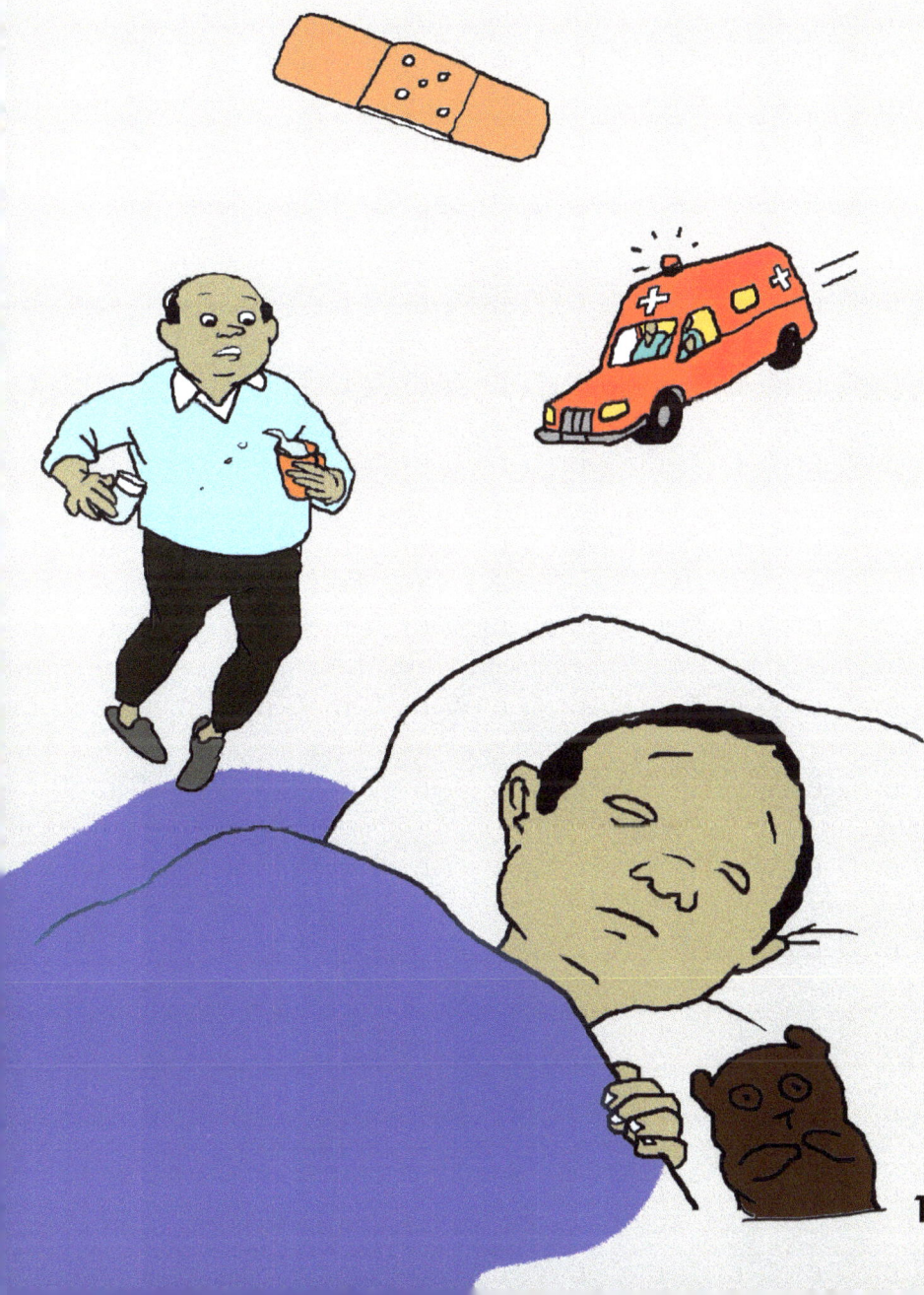

No one is allowed
to bully me or to hit me.

I have the right to play
and to rest.

I have the right to feel safe
and to feel good.

CHILDREN'S RIGHTS

This is your book about children's rights. Everything written here is about you and all the children who are less than 18 years old in the whole world.

Here you will find ten rights. These rights come from the UN Convention on the Rights of the Child. This lists all your rights. And there are lots of other rights that also belong to you too!

A convention is something that many countries have agreed. By signing a convention the country promises to do what is written in it.

Almost all the countries in the world have signed the Convention.

You can use these questions to talk about this book with your family, friends and teachers.

What did you learn from this book?

Describe this book in one word. Funny? Scary? Colourful? Interesting?

How did this book make you feel when you finished reading it?

What was your favourite part of this book?

download our reader app
getlibraryforall.org

About the contributors

Library For All works with authors and illustrators from around the world to develop diverse, relevant, high quality stories for young readers. Visit libraryforall.org for the latest news on writers' workshop events, submission guidelines and other creative opportunities.

Did you enjoy this book?

We have hundreds more expertly curated original stories to choose from.

We work in partnership with authors, educators, cultural advisors, governments and NGOs to bring the joy of reading to children everywhere.

Did you know?

We create global impact in these fields by embracing the United Nations Sustainable Development Goals.

libraryforall.org

www.ingramcontent.com/pod-product-compliance
Lightning Source LLC
Chambersburg PA
CBHW040316050426

42452CB00018B/2864

9 781922 827562